T0157603

THE PREDESTINATION SALVATION PLAN OF CHRIST

WAYNE PHILLIP ARENDSE
AND
EDWARD DIPPENAAR

Order this book online at www.trafford.com
or email orders@trafford.com

Most Trafford titles are also available at major online book retailers.

Printed in the United States of America.

ISBN: 978-1-4669-1722-4 (sc)
ISBN: 978-1-4669-1723-1 (e)

Trafford rev. 03/30/2012

 www.trafford.com

North America & international
toll-free: 1 888 232 4444 (USA & Canada)
phone: 250 383 6864 ♦ fax: 812 355 4082

When *Reading this Book,* it is <u>Very, Very Important,</u> to <u>Understand</u> that this is, Not <u>The Bible</u>, nor <u>The Koran</u>, or <u>The Tora</u> or <u>Any Religious Book</u>. But it's *The Book the Life of Jesus The Second Adam, Soul Body Of Christ. in Revealing* unto Us, in *Him* there is <u>No Religion</u>, <u>No Church</u>, <u>No Nation</u>, <u>No Heaven or Hell</u>, <u>No Right or Wrong</u>, in other words. <u>No Judgement</u> which Refers to <u>Jesus The Saviour</u> who is <u>Son Of Man</u>, the <u>Image Of God.</u>

But now, from *Him* we Have been made *<u>Free,</u>* No more <u>Son Of Man</u>, But now, *Man Of Earth,* in following *The Soul Body* Within Us is, *The Prince Of Peace.*

in this Order we will be able to know

<u>Who We Are,</u>
<u>Where We Come From,</u>
<u>And Where We Are Going Too.</u>

Now Who Are We

We from the Beginning and unto the End the Creation, the <u>Image of Jesus The Saviour, Son of Man the Church of God</u> . . .

Where Do We Come From

When it is said, come let <u>Us Make Man Into Our Image.</u>

And Where Are We Going Too

Back where we <u>Originate</u> Came from, <u>Mother Earth Eve</u>.

and the <u>End</u> of the <u>3-Hours of total darkness</u> of the <u>End</u> of the <u>Creation of life</u> . . .

The <u>Triangle Cycle</u> is from <u>Birth to life</u>, and from *<u>Life to Death.</u>*

<u>Now in order for the Work to take place, this is what happened.</u>

<u>In the Beginning</u>, when <u>God Created Everythhlg in 6 Days</u>, <u>t</u>hat <u>can</u>, <u>an not</u> be seen, was when <u>Time Started.</u>

Now the <u>Creation</u> was <u>Created in Three Parts</u>.

1st: **Water,** The Sea World, was the Spirit of Life, is Death.

2nd: **Earth and Water**, man was one, Woman.

3rd: **Heaven**, Dove and the Word, Two was One.

God the Dove, and the Word Satan.

Which means, the Flesh of the Fish, was the Spirit of Life.

The Flesh of the Beast. was the Son of God. *And the Flesh of the Bird, was the. Dove God, and the Word, the Father Satan.*

The meaning of the WordTripple Six, was the Triangle, Life as we know it was not complete. Three became One, <u>Satan was God the father,</u> and <u>God the</u>

Son Jesu5,the <u>Holy Spirit was the Saving Judgement work.</u>

<u>Adam</u> is the tree the <u>Circle of Life</u>, and became the tree of the <u>Righteous Judgement,</u> by Completing the Cycle, was <u>God of the Holy Bible</u>, is to bring Judgement Unto the *Second Soul Adam, is* the *Tree of Life the Body of Christ.*

And the *Third Soul, Jesus the Second Adam,* is the *Book* of *Life, Quickening Spirit* the *Humanity of Souls,* is the *Soul Body* of *Christ.*

Now, the <u>Sending Promise Work</u> was of **Time**; of the <u>Triangle Creation</u>, for the work of the <u>First Soul Lucifer</u>, was <u>God</u>, and the <u>Father Satan</u>, was <u>the Son Jesus the Saviour.</u>

When <u>God</u> Created man, which is the meaning of the name Adam, in saying come let us make Man; Into our image; <u>Immediately the Word Became Flesh</u>, which means, <u>Two was one</u>, <u>Woman Eve, and Adam.</u>

This is how the Foundation, the First Creation of Life started, <u>God in Three Persons</u> is *AdamOutof Eve*, and <u>Out orEve Woman</u>, came the <u>Profits</u>.

And this is when <u>Moses Desire.</u> was to *See* the Face of Truth. In order for this to take place, he was Instructed to stand between the Cleff of the rock. What <u>Moses</u> Saw, and understood, is the <u>Shadow</u>, the *Quickening Spirit* of the' *Blessing* in part of *Christ*.

And by the <u>Law of Judgement</u>, we that are of the First Creation of the Old Man <u>Jesus the Savioul</u> have received of the *Branch,* out of the tree of *Life* the, *Blessing,* in being <u>Reborn</u> *Man of Earth. Jesus the Second Adam.*

Are Free, from: <u>The Flesh of thc Fish, The Flesh of the Beast, and The Flesh of the Bird, God in Three Persons</u> which is of *All* <u>Traditions</u> and <u>Customs</u> of the <u>Church Body, Jesus the Saviour</u> of this World, by the *Prince of Peace, Adam the Quickening Spirit,* through the <u>Process</u> of the <u>Six Blessings</u>

Now on the <u>Cross</u>, when he said it is <u>Finish</u>, meaning of the *First Glory,* is By *The Quickening Spirit Jesus* the *Second Adam,* <u>Bruising the Head of Satan</u>, is <u>Our Father, of The Bible</u> the <u>Old Law of Moses</u> the <u>Old Testament</u>, is by the Forgiveness of the <u>Law of Judgement</u>, the Healing of the Sick, in Wonder

Works of Miracles, Dreams Visions, Prophecy and Revelations.

And only in this Order. That in the Day, of the *First Blessing,* Is the *Sending* of *Son of Man,* into the Womb Baptized unto *Death,* 'So that the work of the <u>Present</u> *Promise work* unto *Son of Man,* is of the *Blessing Fulfilled,* And of *His Order,* is the *Son of Man Governed.*

But now, First Through the *First Blessing:* of the First day; By <u>Entering</u> into this World, of being Sealed unto death Because of the <u>Fall</u> of *<u>Adam</u>* the <u>Old Man of the First Creation by Falling Under Judgement.</u> It actually refers to the <u>Holy Bible</u> as it is <u>Known</u> of man in this <u>Last Days</u>.

Now, this is that <u>Darkness</u> that *The Quickening Spirit,* <u>Delivered</u> *the Second Soul Adam, the Government Body of Souls, Peacemaker* from when it is Said and Spoken of this <u>Darkness</u> in the <u>Last Day</u> by the <u>Glory Good,</u> <u>Knowledge Evil</u>, Is <u>Judgement</u> on the <u>Increase</u>.

Now this is the <u>Darkness</u> that is the <u>Angel of light</u>, in <u>Confessing</u> as long as <u>I Preach</u> and <u>Believe</u> in the name of *Jesus* the *Saviour* and <u>Continue in The Law Of Judgement</u>, I am *Saved*.

Now the Reflection of the <u>Shadow</u>, is the meaning of: <u>Healing of the sick</u>, <u>Wonder Works</u> of <u>Miracles</u> that *Jesus the Saviour* came too do is of the *Liviticle Priesthood*.

Now in the said of <u>David</u> his son, <u>Solomon</u> was Chosen to build a <u>Temple in</u> the time when there was *Peace,* of the *Blessing* the *Quickening Spirit, Who is the Prince* of *Peace* in part, which was in the <u>Arch of the Covenant</u>, Because *Christ* is the *Everlasting Love,* the *Promise in Full, The Image* of *The Father, the Promise Love.*

Now during the <u>Reign</u> of King David, his <u>Desire</u> was to <u>Build</u> a <u>Temple</u> for *Truth* . . . But he was not allowed to do so, because of being a man of <u>War</u> and <u>Shedding</u> of <u>Blood.</u> His Hands was <u>Defiled</u>, meaning that *Christ* is not <u>Contaminated</u> with, The law of Judgement, Wars, Killing and Shedding of Blood, but is the, *Everlasting Love* from the *Pure Love* of *His Father.*

And in this Order is the *Blessing* the Flesh of a man, is Man of Earth: *Second Adam, i*s the *"Book" of Life* Is <u>Above the life of the Beast.,the old Man</u>. (First Adam) And <u>The Beast the Old Man</u>, is <u>below</u> the *Soul Body* is the *Tree* of *Life.* In <u>Saying</u> it is *Finish,* is the *New Order Man* of <u>Earth</u>, is the *Promise Fulfilled.*

Now because of <u>Judgement</u>, the <u>lord God</u> was removed from the presents of *Christ.* That's why, it is <u>written</u>, *Mercy* of *Christ,* out-ways, the <u>Judgement of the Lord God.</u> In so doing is the *Promise* of *Christ,* <u>Judgement</u> is sent to his own kingdom of this world. So that the work of the *Quickening Spirit,* is fulfilled in saying, behold the life of the *Quickening Spirit Mercy and Compassion* is the Judgement of the *Son* of *Man* <u>Removed</u>, in saying, <u>The Work</u> thou gave'st Me to <u>do</u> is <u>Finished.</u>

For when the <u>Son of God Jesus the Saviour</u> was *Crucified by Jesus the Second Adam,* He said, Father has thou <u>Forgotten Me</u>, and there was the total of <u>3hrs of</u>

Complete Darkness, was of Time, which means, The Righteous Judgement of God was Destroyed. But in *Christ* there is No Time. No Beginning Nor End, but is *from Everlasting to Everlasting* of *His Father,* is the Everlasting love

But by Lucifer, of the First Glory. Losing the *Blessing of Christ,* came the Curse, Death Unto the First Birth the Creation of God *Son* of *Man* that Is Entered into this World and by His Disobedience, Is the Beginning and End of His Creation of life, by God lucifer. and Father Satan of this World.

Now through this <u>Great</u> and <u>Almighty Deceptive Glory</u> of Lucifer <u>the Power</u> of Satan, does the Glory of the. <u>Ambassador of Lucifer the Anti-Christ</u>, who is the 'Holy <u>Apostle Office</u>, appears in a form of a <u>Dove,</u> liken as the *Life* of *the Quickening Spirit, w*hich is as a <u>Reservoir Dam</u> of the <u>Son of Man</u> that Entered into this World, is <u>Sealed</u>. unto <u>Death.</u>

Because of the <u>Old Man</u>who is the <u>Son of Man</u>, in <u>FuHilling the Law of Moses</u>, is to <u>Crucify</u> the *Truth,* by continuing in <u>Judgement.</u>

Now out of this <u>Dam Earth, Eve</u> from the <u>Image of Knowledge Good God</u>, and <u>Evil Satan</u>, comes forth <u>All</u> the <u>Pipes</u>, which <u>Represents Every Church</u> out of <u>Every Religion Kindred and Tongue</u>, is <u>Fed</u> unto the <u>Government</u> *Body* of these Churches of this World, who is God, and through His Sending, He has the <u>Whole World</u> in <u>Worshipping Him</u> as the only <u>True</u>

and <u>living God</u> and *Father,* of *Christ,* who is God in three <u>Persons</u>. But the <u>Ambassador</u> of *Christ;* is not of this World, but in this world *Man of Earth"* who is the *Body* of *Souls,* <u>Governed</u> through the *Blessing, Quickening Spirit* to <u>Quicken</u> *Son* of *Man,* through the *Government Body* through the *Life* of *Mercy and Compassion Peacemaker, who is the Book* of *Life.* Who is <u>Present, of Christ His Father.</u>

In Earth, the <u>Marriage</u> between the <u>Knowledge of Satan, and Glory</u> of <u>God</u> is <u>God the Father (the old man),</u> is *Adam.* The Father of the Whole Humanity of the <u>First Creation Eve. God the Mother Eve, life the Holy Spirit.(Jesus the Saviour)</u> Who is The Image of God. Is *Son* of *Man* . . .

<u>And God the Son, Moses Judgement,</u> Is <u>Worshiped</u> and <u>Loved Throughout</u>the <u>World,</u> for <u>Their Love</u> towards <u>Their belief,</u> by the Power and Glory through God the <u>Holy Spirit, Lucifer the Anti-Christ,</u> appears by the Power of the <u>Government Body</u> of <u>Churches</u> through the Glory of the Emblem of the Dove as the <u>QUickening Spirit</u> by Preaching the <u>Fact is the lie,</u> . . . and <u>the lie is the Fact.</u>

Now the *Truth,* is to Crucify the Judgement of Son of Man by the *Life of the Quickening Spirit* by *Jesus the Second Adam* who is the Ufe of Christ. And the fact is the Lie, Judgement; in fulfilling the Law of Moses in Crucifying Upside Down the Triangle Alpha and Cycle Omega. the *Truth,* the *Quickening Spirit Government Body* of *Paul Mouth* out of the *Truth,* Quickening Spirit is the *True Light* But the (Church Heaven), Heaven Come from Angel Son of Man or !Though, when it is said Creation of Time in his Lucifer this actually refers to Another Gospel and bring you Accursed be let Him, Gospel which is not another, Whole Humanity of the Hearts the Darkened have that Darkness tha and this is Through of His Father to build a Temple for him Christ is Sent that Believing in, *Serve Truth* that he can, man believes, Deception this *by his goodness and has the, Satan who is, God And this is how in his heart-with righteousness, in Spying to Jesus the Second Adam, Palm of his hands in the Whole World.* All these *Soul Body of Christ* the All to You II Give them and I, e.ip M~Wors All Mine are (Churches) Kingdoms to this *Present* always *is, The Quickening Spirit* why Purpose Therefore the, s why That Perverse World and Dark Old Man of the

Will and Not the, *The Will of His Father Christ*, Is to Fulfil the <u>Jesus the Saviour Crucify</u> to *Jnd Adam: Jesus The Sec* is *The Father* of <u>The Will</u> of the <u>Good and the Knowledge, Glory Judgement</u>, <u>Breaking Down the Temple of Solomon</u> in <u>Old Order</u> the, <u>Law of Moses</u> in the *Present Promise Work of Christ* by the, *New Order* the *Resurrecting* and in *0oul Body S, Quickening Spirit, Constitution*f, *Christ Peacemaker* who is the *Son of Man* is, *Work of Promise* by the, *Mercy and Compassion* <u>Judgement of God</u> from the <u>Whole Humanity Saved</u> in <u>The Father</u> of <u>Will</u> the <u>Fulfils</u> *The Quickening Spirit* And in this Order *Darkness have I ca Saying out of His, Son* my *ed* <u>Son of Man</u> man has always believed that he can, <u>Deception of Satan by God</u> But through the <u>Traditions of Holy Days in accordance with Customs</u> in *Truth* Worship the and in this Order, <u>Hearts</u> Their within <u>Their Rituals by the Goodness and Righteousness</u> *Christ of Image* the, *The Quickening Spirit* <u>Worshiping</u> that they are <u>All Believe Their own Beliefs</u> in <u>His Own Sight</u> in <u>Righteous</u> is <u>Ways of Every Man</u> the <u>Written</u> As it is Believe <u>Christian Churctres</u> the, For instance in the name <u>Preach</u> that as long as they <u>Judgement</u> they are free from, *Jesus the Saviour* So does the rest of the other <u>Singing in Songs of Praise</u> and <u>Worshippers Confess in Charismatic Dancing Prophesying,</u> <u>Dreams. Miracles Wonder Works of</u> in <u>Believe</u> and there are those who that this is done by the <u>Declare</u> *Sun Under* the <u>Every Church Visions</u> and *Life of The Quickening Spirit*

The Sealing of the Dead as it is known of the Churches, Is the Sealing of Death unto *Son* of *Man* is the Closing of the Gates of Hell. It is Believed Throughout the Churches, who is the Church Body of Jesus the Saviour of this World, that in Partaking the Sacrament is the Forgiveness of Judgement.

Not so, but to Continue in Judgement. And this is how the Whole World is being, Deceived by the Power of Satan and the Glory of God, in Continuing Believing in Partaking the Sacrament is the Forgiveness of Judgement. *Worthily* is to Partake it Once and for All, Unworthily is to Partake it throughout one's life, and that is how *Son* of *Man* continues In Judgement . . . By Believing in receiving the Holy Spirit and Continuing in Judgement, there is no Forgiveness, Which refers to the New Testament Holy Spirit of the Glory God and the Old Testament Is the Judgement, the Curse that came upon Lucifer in Receiving the Name Devil or Satan is to Continue in Judgement and it is known as the Holy Bible and this Is through the Glory God, is the Gates of Hell open and by the Power of Satan Closed. In this Order, is the *True* Meaning of the Sealing of Death unto *Son* of *Man*.

Now, the Blessing of All Churches, Religions, Nations, Kindred and tongues, is the Church Body Jesus the Saviour . . . I build my church in this order, follow me as I follow in Obtaining Power, Judgement and Glory ofthis World, is to Continue in the Life of the Old man *of* Judgement, by Believing In *Jesus the Saviour,* when it is said, unto Thee Give I the Keys . . .

What Thou Open in earth (Hell), is Opened in Heaven, (the Church Heaven). What Thou Loosen in Earth is Loosened in Heaven, and what Thou Bind in Earth is bound in Heaven . . . Meaning, the Healing of the Head is the Power and Gi.ory of Lucifer.

In the *Presents of Christ,* the Two Souls of *Chrisl is:*

The First Soul, of the Sending Work Lucifer, And the *Second Soul, is the Present Work Adam*.

In Earth, in <u>Crucifying upside down</u> through <u>Jesus the Saviour</u>, which means by the Power of Satan. <u>Jesus the Saviour</u> means <u>Rock, Power, Judgement and Glory</u> of *Paradise* of this World. which is the <u>Glory of Lucifer</u>.

That is why the *Blessing* of *Christ* is referred to the *Second Adam, <u>Out of Darkness have I Called Mv Son</u>.* (Of the Old Man.) Now in the *Presents* of *Christ,* the *Promise* of <u>*The Father*</u> is, the *Blessing* of *The Quickening Spirit.* In the *Blessing; Second Adam,* the *Body* of *Quickening Souls,* is the *Body* of *Christ.*

As it is <u>Written</u>, Satan the <u>Head of Hell</u>in Earth, which means, in <u>Tempting Man</u>, to bring <u>Suffering, Sorrow and.</u> Destruction, which Leads to the Judgement of *Son* of *Man* of the <u>Whole Humanity</u>in this World. God, the Head of <u>Heaven (Church Heaven)</u> in Earth to <u>Imprison</u> *Son* of *Man* in <u>Their Different</u> Beliefs, in <u>Deceiving</u> them by Believing that they are All Worshiping the *Only True* and <u>Living God</u>, of which the truth is, the <u>Devil</u>, who is <u>God</u>.

As it Written, <u>Through God</u> He is <u>Able</u>to <u>Cause Fire</u> to come Down from the <u>Heavens (Churches)</u> which is the <u>Emblem of the Holy Spirit</u>, and that is how <u>He has All</u> the <u>Churches in</u> the <u>Palm of His hand</u>, in Worshipping these Days as it is Celebrated Once a Year: <u>Good Friday</u>, in <u>Burying One's Sins in the Open Grave</u>, Ascension <u>Day</u>, <u>Pentecostal Day</u>, <u>Father</u> and <u>Mothers Day</u>, <u>Christmas Day</u>, etc. And this is known as <u>Holy Days</u>, but the truth is that, these are <u>all Celebrations</u> of <u>Paganism</u>, <u>by Worshipping Satan Unknowingly</u> . . . Today it is known and Referred to The different <u>Nations</u>of this World of their great powers, but there is no. Greater <u>Power</u>than the <u>Knowledge</u> of the Churches through the <u>Power of Deceptiveness</u>, and that is to <u>Preach</u> that the *Fact* is a <u>Lie</u>, and <u>the Lie</u> is *the Fact,* and that is how the Death of The *Son* of *Man* is being Sealed by the Closing of the gates <u>of Hell</u>in Believing as long as <u>I Believe in *Jesus* the *Saviour*</u> and <u>Continue in the Law of Judgement</u>, <u>I am Saved</u> by Partaking of the <u>Sacrament</u>, the <u>Holy Communion</u> of the <u>Body and Blood</u>of *Jesus,* the <u>Saviour</u> and this is, How <u>God Receives Glory</u>, and <u>Satan Power</u> *over the Son* of *Man* of the Churches of this World, the <u>Kingdom of God</u> who Appears as *Jesus Christ* within the <u>Hearts</u> of men.

Now this is what is meant when the <u>Wound of his Head</u> is Healed . . . Satan did not only <u>Receive Power</u> of Hell, but also the <u>Glory of God of Heaven</u>.

But the Churches Believe is to Continue in this way. The <u>Church Leaders</u>, who is the <u>Apostle. Pope</u>, or any <u>Other leader</u> has the <u>Power</u> to <u>Open</u> the <u>Gates</u> of <u>Hell</u> and to <u>Close</u> it, so that *Son* of *Man* may Enter into <u>Heaven.(the Church Heaven)</u>.

Of Earth, in Crucifying in part <u>Upright</u> is the *Promise of Christ*. Which means <u>*Brother*</u> *Paul Second Adam* in Crucifying, in saying <u>*I Die Daily*</u> to *Arise* in the *New Order* to *Enter Unto* the *<u>Everlasting Love, Christ</u>*, By signifying to' <u>Jesus the Saviour</u>, the <u>Apostle of Lucifer' On Earth, Paradise, Judgement of the Old Man Death</u>. *And Brother Paul the Blessing* of *Christ, Man* of *Earth, Blessing* of *the New Promise is Christ, Life.'* <u>Our Father: Satan of Lucifer</u>, and *Adam,* the *Tree of Life* who is the <u>Sons</u> of the *Body of Souls of Christ*. But *My Father* is the Soul Body of *Christ,* the *Son* of the *Everlasting Father.*

I am *the Truth the Way and the Life, Quickening Soul, Peacemaker.* When itwas <u>Prophesied,</u> in the <u>Last days</u> through the <u>Knowledge of Good Is Judgement</u> on the <u>Increase.</u>

And this is the Five Wounds of the Crucifixion of the *Government Body, Peacemaker of the.* Cross, the Judgement unto *Son of Man.* The Four Wounds is the Blessing, the *Body of Souls,* and' the Fifth is the *Quickening Spirit,* the *Body of Quickening SoWs, Peacemaker,* and this is the Explanation of the Word *Christ Jesus* the *Second Adam* (After the Crucifixion)

But the Judgement of Saul of the Old Man, to *Brother Paul,* the Blessing of the Young Man, is *Follow Me* as *I Follow* the *Quickening Spirit,* in Crucifying the Judgement of *Son of Man* through the *Quickening Spirit,* is to Crucify the Judgement of the Heart in *Following The Quickening Spirit,* to Fulfill in Removing the head of Satan through the Five Blessings of the *Government Body, Peacemaker:*

In so doing, fulfilling the *Blessing* of the *Quickening Souls, Peacemaker,* Is the Promise, After the Order of the New Constitution, Is the *Malkisadek Priesthood,* *i*n order so that this Promise work can take place in the *Presents of Christ* the *'Everlasting Love of the Father. The Body of Christ the Prince of Peace, the Body of the Peacemaker, Quickening Spirit.*

Now the Third Soul, Jesus the Second Adam, is the *Soul Body 'of Christ, Man of Earth.* The *Promise Work* of the *Father is The Quickening Spirit,* to CruCify the <u>Old Man,</u> <u>Jesus the Saviour</u> the <u>Law of Judgement</u> and in fulfilling the *Blessing* of the *Father Christ . . .* <u>Was Jesus the Saviour Son of Man on the Cross,</u> *Is the Promise Work of Christ fulfilled.*

Thus freeing <u>Son of Man</u> from the <u>Righteous Judgement,</u> <u>The Image of God</u>. In Giving <u>Son of Man</u> the *Blessing* of the *Second Birth, Man* of *Earth,* The *Quickening Spirit in Part the Prince of Peace, is Jesus the Second Adam.*

For this is the *Blessing* that's been given by the *Promise Work* unto *Son of Man*

ls the *Quickening Spirit* is *Mercy and Compassion,* and from *Mercy and Compassion* to *Man* of *Earth* in Following, the <u>*Prince of Peace is the Soul Body of Christ.*</u>

(1) Now *Re-incarnation* is the <u>CyCle</u>.

(2) <u>The Cycle</u> is *The Body of Souls.*

(3) *The Body of Souls* is the *Tree of Life.*

(4) And the *Tree of Life* is the *Soul Body of Christ.*

(5) *The Soul Body of Christ* is *The Quickening Spirit.*

(6) *The Quickening Spirit* is to <u>Re-incarnate</u> the *Body of Souls unto Christ,* is the <u>Circle Complete.</u>

Is By *The Quickening Spirit* Fulfilling <u>All blessings</u> *is the promise of Christ Fulfilled.*

The Flesh of a man, is the *Soul Body Adam the Tree of Life,* that <u>Entered</u> into the <u>Body of Adam and Eve,</u> who is <u>Son of Man</u> was <u>to Complete the CyCle.</u> Except for the <u>third</u> *Soul* was kept the *Book of Life is Jesus the Second Adam,* so that, the *Process is Fulfilled.*

The Present Promise Work, Truth is *Jesus the _second Adam, Soul Body of Christ* In <u>Crucifying not Without,</u> But *Within* the <u>Creation from the Beginning to the End of Life,</u> Was the <u>First Adam the Breathe of Life, Jesus the Saviour the Image of God.</u>

Follow *Of Me, The Prince of Peace* Within You.

Is the *Quickening Spirit* of the *Second Birth,* is the *Jesus the Second Adam,* In saying . . . *I'm Truth, I'm the Way, I'm the Book of Life.* Is the <u>Foundation,</u> of the *Present Promise Work* of the *Soul Body of Christ.* Is, *The Life* where there is <u>No, Time, No Beginning Nor End, No Church, No Religion, No Tradition, Customs, Holy days, Countries, Nations,</u> In other words, <u>No Son of Man,</u> <u>Who is Jesus the Saviour the Image of God,</u> But now *Man of Earth, Jesus the*

Second Adam'the _Blessing_ is the _Promise Christ,_ _i_s the _NEW DA_ Y. _The Life of the Everlasting Father._ And thus being able to say, <u>No More Our Father</u>, but _My Father:_

Printed in the United States
By Bookmasters